# Contents

# Introduction

If you are wild about learning and wild about animals, this book is for you! It will take you on a wild adventure, where you will practise key maths skills and explore the amazing world of sea animals along the way.

Each maths topic is introduced in a clear and simple way, with lots of interesting activities to complete, so that you can practise what you have learned.

You should attempt the tasks without a calculator unless instructed otherwise, but calculators may be used to check your answers.

Alongside every maths topic, you will discover fascinating facts about sea creatures. The animals in this hugely diverse group live in, on or by the world's seas and oceans. What is your favourite sea creature?

When you have completed each topic, record the animals that you have seen and the skills that you have learned in the explorer's logbook on pages 44–45.

Good luck, explorer! Try not to get too wet!

**Pamela Wild**

# Place value

## WILD FACT

The blue whale has no teeth. Instead, it has 320 comb-like plates in its mouth that can sieve 5000 kg of water and plankton in one mouthful.

The blue whale is the giant of the ocean. You may be amazed to learn though, that it only eats plankton – the smallest of creatures.

A number can only be made up from the digits 1–9 and zero, and its value depends upon the column each digit is in.

Order these numbers from smallest to biggest:

| 7612 | 701 | 76012 | 67233 | 671001 |
|------|-----|-------|-------|--------|
| **701** | **7612** | **67233** | **76012** | **671001** |

## FACT FILE

**Animal:** Blue whale
**Habitat:** Almost all the world's oceans
**Weight:** 181400 kg (av.)
**Lifespan:** 80 to 90 years
**Diet:** Small crustaceans called krill

## Task 1  Write these numbers in figures.

a  one million _100,0000_

b  eight hundred and fifty thousand and five _850005_

c  forty-six thousand four hundred and sixty _46460 6_

## Task 2  Write these numbers in words.

a  178,000 _one hundred and seventy eight thousand._

b  904,390 _nine hundred and four thousend three hundred and ninty._

2

**Task 3**  Order these numbers from biggest to smallest.

**a** 909 009          990 009          999 090          990 090          991 099

_999 090, 991 099, 990 090, 990 009 and_

**b** 785 642          758 246          786 462          758 462          786 463

_____

Order these numbers from smallest to biggest.

**c** 505 005          550 505          555 050          555 555          505 055

_____

**d** 100 304          100 004          100 403          101 001          10 999

_____

**Task 4**  Fill in the gaps in the number sequences.

**a** _____    9246    9146    _____    _____    8846    _____

**b** 435 653    _____    635 653    735 653    _____    _____    _____

## WILD FACT

There used to be hundreds of thousands of blue whales in our oceans. Now, there are fewer than 10 000 left.

**Exploring Further ...**

**a** The average length of a blue whale is twenty-five thousand millimetres. Write this number in figures: _____

**b** The greatest weight recorded was 177 998, 176 999 or 177 989 kg. Write the largest of these numbers here: _____ kg

**c** Another whale weighed thirty thousand kilograms less than this. Work out its weight and write it here: _____ kg

**Now dive to pages 44–45 to record what you have learned in your explorer's logbook.**

3

# Rounding numbers

**Rounding** numbers to the nearest 10, 100, 1000, 10 000 or 100 000 can make them easier to manage and understand, especially if we are unable to be, or do not want to be, exact. Rounding a number enables us to estimate accurately.

The breeding ground of the emperor penguin may contain about 25 000 birds. It is more sensible to say '25 000' than '25 359' because we would probably never be able to find out the exact number. Therefore, 25 000 has been rounded to the nearest thousand and includes any number from 24 500 to 25 499.

As well as rounding numbers, you need to be able to work with negative numbers – an important skill in the below-freezing temperatures of the Antarctic!

## FACT FILE

**Animal:** Emperor penguin
**Habitat:** The ice and waters of the Antarctic
**Weight:** 22 to 40 kg
**Lifespan:** Up to 20 years
**Diet:** Squid, krill and fish

---

**Task 1**    Round these numbers to the nearest ten.

a 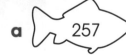 257 _____     b  134 443 _____

**Round these numbers to the nearest hundred.**

c 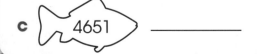 4651 _____     d  17 749 _____

**Task 2**   Round these numbers to the nearest thousand.

a  3611 _____   b  54 001 _____

Round these numbers to the nearest ten thousand.

c 45 000 _____   d 8674 _____

**Task 3**   Round these numbers to the nearest hundred thousand.

a 145 612 _____

b 250 006 _____

**Task 4**

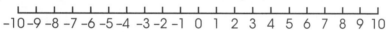
–10 –9 –8 –7 –6 –5 –4 –3 –2 –1 0 1 2 3 4 5 6 7 8 9 10

a What is the difference between 8 and –6? _____

b What is –4 + 7? _____

c The temperature is 9° and then drops by 11°.

What is the new temperature? _____

**WILD FACT**

The female lays a single egg but leaves it with the male, who keeps it warm on his feet for most of the incubation period. 'Mum' goes off to feed, leaving 'Dad' in the wind and the cold, and without food!

**Exploring Further ...**

Write the range of numbers which could be included in the following statements, e.g. A penguin's egg is incubated for about 50 days. Range (to nearest 10) = 45 to 54 days

a The emperor penguin stays under water for about 10 minutes.

Range (to nearest 10) = _____ to _____ mins

b An emperor penguin may swim about 100 km to reach a suitable breeding ground.

Range (to nearest 100) = _____ to _____ km

c There are about 150 000 pairs of emperor penguins in the Antarctic.

Range (to nearest 10 000) = _____ to _____ pairs

**Now sledge to pages 44–45 to record what you have learned in your explorer's logbook.**

# Addition

Adding increases whole positive numbers. You can add mentally (in your head) or by using the **columnar method**. When using the latter method, make sure you put the digits in the correct columns.

Since 1910, the number of sea otters in the wild has increased from about 2000 by 98 000, making a total population of about 100 000.

## Task 1 — Work out these sums in your head.

a Calculate 38 plus 43 _____

b Increase 87 by 54 _____

c What is 8721 plus 1268? _____

d 416 + 57 _____

e Add together 804 and 296 _____

**WILD FACT**

The sea otter has developed an ingenious way of eating – by using its chest as a table! It uses a stone to smash awkward shells on its chest.

**WILD FACT**

The sea otter has a big appetite, eating up to one-quarter of its body weight in food per day! In between feeds, it sleeps on its back, either with its front legs folded on its chest or with its paws over its eyes. What a cutie!

**FACT FILE**

**Animal:** Sea otter
**Habitat:** Around the coasts of the northern Pacific Ocean
**Weight:** Up to 30 kg
**Lifespan:** Up to 23 years
**Diet:** Fish, shellfish, squid, crabs and octopus

Solve these problems in your head.

**a** A sea otter's head and body measure 55 cm and its tail is 15 cm long.

What is its total length? _____

**b** Two sea otters weigh 38 kg and 27 kg respectively.

What is their combined weight? _____

**c** Sea otters often dive to a depth of 18 m but one dived a further 77 m.

How deep did this particular otter dive? _____

Work out the answers here using the columnar method.

**a** In 1910 there were 487 sea otters off the coast of Japan. This number has increased by 24 523. How many otters are there now?

**b** Numbers of sea otters around California decreased by 235 to 549 in 1910. How many sea otters were there before 1910?

**Exploring Further ...**

**a** There are 47 683 sea otters along the Pacific coastline of Alaska and Canada and 39 578 along the Pacific coastline of the USA. How many are there altogether along these coastlines?

_____

**b** There are a further 17 299 otters around the coastlines of Japan and eastern Russia. How many sea otters are there in total?

_____

**c** Check your answers by rounding all the figures to the nearest thousand.

_____

**Now float to pages 44–45 to record what you have learned in your explorer's logbook.**

# Subtraction

**Subtracting**
helps us to compare how much bigger, wider, further or heavier one animal, person, thing or place is than another. When you subtract whole positive numbers, your answer will be less than what you started with. And always remember to subtract the smaller number from the bigger one!

**Task 1**   Work out these problems in your head.

a Decrease 85 by 42 _____

b Find the difference between 457 and 689 _____

c Subtract 440 from 2980 _____

d 463 – 48                _____

e 657 – 83                _____

f 341 – 159               _____

g How much greater is 121 than 55? _____

h Take away 97 from 333            _____

i What is 57 less than 525?        _____

**Task 2**  Work out these problems in your head.

a The wingspan of an albatross is 350 cm. A herring gull's is 174 cm.

What is the difference between the two? _____

b 9500 km – ⬜ = 7479 km

c 85 500 + ⬜ = 87 250

**WILD FACT**

The female albatross lays a single egg. It takes 78 days to hatch and the chick takes a further 278 days to fledge.

**Task 3**  Complete these sums using the columnar method.

a
```
    590
  - 327
  _____

  _____
```

b
```
   9427
  - 7295
  _____

  _____
```

c
```
  37 821
 - 21 949
 _____

 _____
```

d
```
   84 067
  - 69 295
  _____

  _____
```

e
```
  245 100
  - 89 732
  _____

  _____
```

f
```
  500 000
  - 61 158
  _____

  _____
```

**WILD FACT**

This mighty bird can fly 10 000 miles in a single journey without flapping its wings. One tagged bird is known to have flown 6000 miles in just 12 days.

**Exploring Further ...**

A wandering albatross (A) flew 162 423 km, 157 986 km and 96 501 km over a three-year period. His mate (B) flew 143 805 km, 169 037 km and 127 419 km.

a How far did each albatross fly? A: _____ B: _____

b Which bird flew further? _____

c By how much? _____

**Now glide to pages 44–45 to record what you have learned in your explorer's logbook.**

# Number knowledge

Discover whether you have a nose for numbers as you leap through **multiples**, **factors**, **prime**, **square** and **cube** numbers!

For example, there is a pod of 36 dolphins.

36:
- is not a prime number
- is even
- is a square number ($6 \times 6 = 36$)
- has factors of 36 and 1, 2 and 18, 3 and 12, 4 and 9, and 6
- has multiples including 72, 108 and 144
- is a multiple of 18, 12, 9, 6, 4, 3, 2 and 1.

## Task 1 — Underline the numbers which are ...

a  Multiples of 8:              14  22  38  56  48  96

b  Multiples of 7:              35  63  49  57  73  21

c  Multiples of both 9 and 6:  15  54  72  18  66  36

d  Multiples of both 4 and 3:  18  16  12  32  28  24

## WILD FACT

Bottlenose dolphins communicate with one another through a series of clicks and whistling calls. They are very caring towards one another, rushing to help an injured dolphin and acting as very good 'midwives' too.

## FACT FILE

**Animal:** Bottlenose dolphin
**Habitat:** Temperate and tropical oceans around the world
**Weight:** 500 kg
**Lifespan:** 20 to 40 years
**Diet:** Crustaceans, squid, shrimp and small fish

**Task 2** Write down all the factors of the following numbers. Remember to include the number itself and 1.

a  18 _____

b  32 _____

Write down the factors common to both numbers.

c  36 and 24 _____

**Task 3**  Now try these.

a  Underline the square numbers:     6      66      36      64      47      4

b  Underline the cube numbers:     115     100     1000     8     64     16

c  Underline the prime numbers:     37      51      29      97      2      91

Fill in the gaps with a number from 2–8 to make both sides of the equation equal.

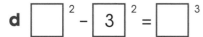

d  $\boxed{\phantom{x}}^2 - \boxed{3}^2 = \boxed{\phantom{x}}^3$

e  $\boxed{5}^2 - \boxed{\phantom{x}}^2 = \boxed{\phantom{x}}^2$

**Exploring Further ...**

The answers to the sums on either side of the equals sign should be the same. Investigate whether these are correct or incorrect .

e.g. $4 \times 35 = 2 \times 2 \times 5 \times 7$ CORRECT

Where they are incorrect, correct the sum on the right of the equals sign.

a  $9 \times 15 = 3^2 \times 5$        _____

b  $2 \times 80 = 4^2 \times 10$        _____

c  $25 \times 10 = 2 \times 5^2$        _____

d  $12 \times 360 = 4 \times 3 \times 9 \times 10$        _____

e  $54 \times 18 = 3^2 \times 6^2$        _____

**Now leap to pages 44–45 to record what you have learned in your explorer's logbook.**

# Multiplication

**Multiplication** is a quick way to add up. Multiply means 'sets of'.

For example: 5 × 7 means 5 sets of 7.

Discover how quickly you can recall your times tables facts then investigate more formal written methods, e.g. **long multiplication**.

**Task 1**  Multiply these sums in your head.

**a** **i)** 3 × 4 _____  **ii)** 7 × 2 _____  **iii)** 8 × 3 _____  **iv)** 9 × 4 _____

**b** **i)** 7 × 5 _____  **ii)** 9 × 6 _____  **iii)** 3 × 5 _____  **iv)** 4 × 6 _____

**c** **i)** 8 × 7 _____  **ii)** 7 × 7 _____  **iii)** 9 × 8 _____  **iv)** 5 × 8 _____

**d** **i)** 3 × 9 _____  **ii)** 7 × 9 _____  **iii)** 6 × 8 _____  **iv)** 6 × 7 _____

**Task 2**  Solve these problems using a formal written method.

**a** The average weight of one seahorse is 7g. What is the total weight of 198 seahorses?

**b** A seahorse can produce 50 young. How many young will nine seahorses produce?

**Use a formal written method to find the answers to these sums.**

**a  i)** 47 × 5 **ii)** 807 × 6 **iii)** 8206 × 8

**b  i)** 86 × 9 **ii)** 270 × 4 **iii)** 9579 × 2

**Use long multiplication to discover the answers to these sums.**

**c  i)** 67 × 58 **ii)** 106 × 86 **iii)** 4790 × 75

## FACT FILE

| | |
|---|---|
| **Animal:** | Seahorse |
| **Habitat:** | Shallow temperate and tropical shores around the world |
| **Weight:** | Up to 140 g |
| **Lifespan:** | 1 to 5 years |
| **Diet:** | Small crustaceans and plankton |

## WILD FACT

Seahorses' eyes can swivel, which means they can turn their eyes without moving their bodies. When prey is within reach, they swiftly snatch it or suck it into their beak-like mouths.

### Exploring Further ...

A seahorse's dorsal fin beats 35 times per second. Investigate how many times it will beat in:

**a**  one minute _____

**b**  75 seconds _____

**c**  one hour  _____

**Now hover down to pages 44–45 to record what you have learned in your explorer's logbook.**

# Fractions

Do you know that **equivalent fractions** have different **numerators** (the number on the top) and **denominators** (the number on the bottom), yet represent the same amount?

For example: $\frac{1}{4}$ of a whale pod and $\frac{2}{8}$ of the same whale pod are exactly the same size.

**Improper fractions** are 'top heavy' – the numerator is bigger than the denominator.

For example: $\frac{5}{2}$ is improper.

A **mixed number** includes a whole number and a fraction.

For example: $2\frac{1}{2}$

**Task 1** Make equivalent fractions using the fractions wall to help you.

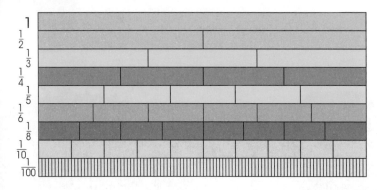

**a i)** $\frac{1}{2} = \frac{\phantom{0}}{4}$ **ii)** $\frac{3}{4} = \frac{6}{\phantom{0}}$ **iii)** $\frac{4}{5} = \frac{\phantom{0}}{.0}$ **iv)** $\frac{4}{6} = \frac{2}{\phantom{0}}$

**b** $\frac{1}{2} = \frac{\phantom{0}}{4} = \frac{\phantom{0}}{6} = \frac{\phantom{0}}{8} = \frac{\phantom{0}}{10} = \frac{\phantom{0}}{100}$ **c** $\frac{1}{4} = \frac{\phantom{0}}{8} = \frac{\phantom{0}}{100}$

**d** Put = , > or < into the gaps below.

**i)** $\frac{1}{2} \quad \frac{4}{5}$ **ii)** $\frac{7}{8} \quad \frac{8}{10}$ **iii)** $\frac{3}{4} \quad \frac{75}{100}$

= means 'equals'
< means 'less than'
> means 'more than'

**Task 2** Change these improper fractions into mixed numbers.

a i) $\dfrac{7}{5}$  ii) $\dfrac{9}{6}$

Change these mixed numbers into improper fractions.

b i) $1\dfrac{3}{4}$  ii) $2\dfrac{4}{5}$

**Task 3** Work out these fractions sums.

a i) $\dfrac{1}{5} + \dfrac{2}{5} =$  ii) $\dfrac{3}{6} + \dfrac{4}{6} =$

b i) $\dfrac{7}{9} - \dfrac{5}{9} =$  ii) $\dfrac{6}{7} - \dfrac{3}{7} =$

Find the lowest common denominator and add or subtract.

c i) $\dfrac{2}{5} + \dfrac{3}{10} =$  ii) $\dfrac{7}{8} + \dfrac{3}{4} =$

d i) $\dfrac{8}{15} - \dfrac{2}{5} =$  ii) $\dfrac{8}{9} - \dfrac{1}{3} =$

**WILD FACT**

The sperm whale can dive to depths of 3000 m, staying under water for about three-quarters (spot the fraction!) of an hour.

**Exploring Further ...**

The grids shown represent 2 whole ones.
Each has been divided into thirty-sixths.

On the first grid:

a i) Shade $\dfrac{1}{6}$  ii) Now shade $\dfrac{5}{12}$

iii) Now shade $\dfrac{2}{9}$  iv) Now shade $\dfrac{7}{36}$

On the second grid:

v) Shade $\dfrac{5}{18}$  vi) Now shade $\dfrac{1}{3}$

vii) Now shade $\dfrac{5}{36}$

b How much has been shaded on the two grids? _____

c How much is unshaded? _____

**Now swim to pages 44–45 to record what you have learned in your explorer's logbook.**

**Division** means sharing, or finding out how many sets of one number there are in another.

For example: 16 ÷ 4 would mean 16 sweets shared equally between 4 people, or how many sets of four there are in 16.

If the sum does not divide equally, you must be able to deal with the remainder.

For example: $15 \div 4 = 3 \text{ r } 3 = 3\frac{3}{4} = 3.75$

Occasionally, the problem will require you to round the remainder.

## FACT FILE

**Animal:** Giant octopus

**Habitat:** The coast of the northern Pacific Rim and some coasts of the Southern Hemisphere

**Weight:** 3 to 10kg

**Lifespan:** 3 to 5 years

**Diet:** Crabs, molluscs, squid and crayfish

## WILD FACT

The giant octopus can defend itself from attack by shooting out a thick, ink-like cloud. If that doesn't work, it can change its skin colour. It has a horny beak which can deliver a crushing bite to its prey. Its victims can also be paralysed by poison from its salivary gland.

**Task 1** Answer these sums as quickly as you can.

a i) 28 ÷ 4 = ____    ii) 36 ÷ 3 = ____

b i) 55 ÷ 5 = ____    ii) 12 ÷ 4 = ____

c i) 54 ÷ 6 = ____    ii) 63 ÷ 7 = ____

d i) 45 ÷ 9 = ____    ii) 35 ÷ 7 = ____

e i) 80 ÷ 2 = ____    ii) 64 ÷ 8 = ____

f i) 42 ÷ 6 = ____    ii) 72 ÷ 12 = ____

g i) 27 ÷ 3 = ____    ii) 44 ÷ 11 = ____

h i) 56 ÷ 7 = ____    ii) 12 ÷ 12 = ____

**Task 2**

Use the formal written method of short division to find the answers to these sums. Show any remainders as r 1,2,3 etc.

**a** $735 \div 7$     **b** $7539 \div 2$     **c** $9634 \div 8$

**Task 3**

Investigate how to deal with remainders.

**a** Deep-sea divers are taken out in boats which can hold 6 divers each. How many boats are required for 46 divers?

**b** A baby whale drinks 2450 litres of milk from its mother over the course of 4 days. If it drinks the same amount each day, find out how much is drunk per day. Show your remainder as a fraction.

**WILD FACT**

The giant octopus is the largest of all the invertebrates (creatures that don't have a backbone), having a tentacle span of 7 m and weighing up to 70 kg.

**Exploring Further ...**

Make a two-digit number from each set of numbers and divide by the third number. Organise the numbers to give the biggest possible remainder.

e.g.  3  6  4     $34 \div 6 = 5 \text{ r } 4$
$34 \div 6$ gives the biggest remainder.

**a**  5  2  3

**b**  6  5  4

**c**  4  5  2

**Now sweep to pages 44–45 to record what you have learned in your explorer's logbook.**

# Decimals

A manta ray's width is approximately 2.2 times the length of its body.

**Decimals** are another way of expressing fractions. The decimal point separates the whole number from the fraction or the 'parts of the whole number'.

Just as whole number columns extend to the left, decimal columns extend to the right, in tenths, hundredths and thousandths.

## Task 1 — Explore these sums.

**a** How many tenths in?

   **i)** 2 _____  **ii)** 0.8 _____  **iii)** 35 _____

**b** How many hundredths in?

   **i)** 0.63 _____  **ii)** 0.02 _____  **iii)** 0.4 _____

**c** How many thousandths in?

   **i)** 0.736 _____  **ii)** 0.15 _____  **iii)** 0.6 _____

### FACT FILE

**Animal:** Manta ray
**Habitat:** Tropical, sub-tropical and temperate seas around the world
**Weight:** Up to 1350 kg
**Lifespan:** Up to 20 years
**Diet:** Small fish, crabs, shrimp and plankton

## Task 2 — Round to the nearest whole number.

**a  i)** 830.18 _____  **ii)** 409.73 _____  **iii)** 399.81 _____

Round to one decimal place.

**b  i)** 4.05 _____  **ii)** 8.14 _____  **iii)** 5.98 _____

## Task 3 — Write down these decimals' fractions.

**a i)** 0.1      **ii)** 0.3      **iii)** 0.8

**b i)** 0.37      **ii)** 0.18      **iii)** 0.05

**c i)** 0.951      **ii)** 0.013      **iii)** 0.004

### Write these fractions as decimals.

**d i)** $\dfrac{5}{10}$ _____ **ii)** $\dfrac{4}{10}$ _____ **iii)** $\dfrac{9}{10}$ _____

**e i)** $\dfrac{32}{100}$ _____ **ii)** $\dfrac{56}{100}$ _____ **iii)** $\dfrac{2}{100}$ _____

**f i)** $\dfrac{691}{1000}$ _____ **ii)** $\dfrac{43}{1000}$ _____ **iii)** $\dfrac{6}{1000}$ _____

**WILD FACT**

Imagine being in a small boat when a huge creature leaps out of the water like a giant kite! The manta ray has frightened fishermen in this way so often that it has been nicknamed the "devil fish".

## Task 4 — Write these numbers in figures.

**a i)** eighty-five point eight _____ **ii)** fifty-five hundredths _____

**b i)** eighty tenths _____ **ii)** five hundred and five hundredths _____

### Put these numbers in order from biggest to smallest.

**c** 2.059   2.591   2.008   2.058   2.915

_____

**d** 4.21   3.84   3.9   3.814   3.841

_____

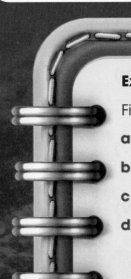

### Exploring Further ...

Find the answers to these sums.

**a**   Subtract 4.8 from 6.5 _____

**b**   Find the difference between 1.25 and 5.3 _____

**c**   5.9 minus 4.7 _____

**d**   Find the total of 3.4 and 4.65 _____

**Now float to pages 44–45 to record what you have learned in your explorer's logbook.**

19

# Percentages

**Per cent**

(%) is another way of expressing a fraction or proportion. It relates to the number of parts per 100, so it's easier than fractions and decimals! Therefore, 57% means 57 out of every hundred. Can you write percentages as a decimal and as a fraction (with a denominator of 100)?

$67\% = 0.67 = \frac{67}{100}$

**Task 1**  Write these percentages as decimals.

a  i) 43% —  ii) 59% —  iii) 40% —  iv) 93% —

b  i) 1% —  ii) 4% —  iii) 7% —  iv) 9% —

Write these decimals as percentages.

c  i) 0.18 —  ii) 0.42 —  iii) 0.68 —  iv) 0.2 —

d  i) 0.02 —  ii) 0.03 —  iii) 0.05 —  iv) 0.06 —

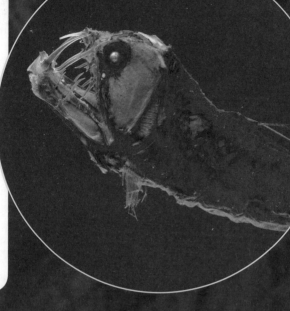

**Task 2**  Write each percentage as a fraction with a denominator of 100.

**a i)** 13%  **ii)** 27%  **iii)** 50%

**b i)** 2%  **ii)** 3%  **iii)** 6%

Write these fractions as percentages.

**c i)** $\frac{15}{100}$ ____  **ii)** $\frac{34}{100}$ ____  **iii)** $\frac{90}{100}$ ____

**d i)** $\frac{4}{100}$ ____  **ii)** $\frac{9}{100}$ ____  **iii)** $\frac{7}{100}$ ____

**Task 3**  Make equivalent fractions and convert to percentages.

**a i)** $\frac{1}{10} = \frac{\square}{100} = \square$ %  **ii)** $\frac{3}{10} = \frac{\square}{100} = \square$ %

**b i)** $\frac{1}{5} = \frac{\square}{10} = \frac{\square}{100} = \square$ %  **ii)** $\frac{4}{5} = \frac{\square}{10} = \frac{\square}{100} = \square$ %

**c i)** $\frac{1}{2} = \frac{\square}{10} = \frac{\square}{100} = \square$ %  **ii)** $\frac{1}{4} = \frac{\square}{100} = \square$ %

**WILD FACT**

Be in no doubt about the viperfish's intentions – here is a very efficient killer! It is only 30 cm long but with the help of its specially adapted teeth (which are angled backwards) and jaws (which it can unhinge) it can swallow prey the same size as itself.

**Exploring Further ...**

**a**   **b**

Put one of the following values into each individual square so that each large square totals 100%.

$\frac{2}{5}$  0.45  $\frac{1}{4}$  10%  0.07  $\frac{1}{5}$  23%  $\frac{3}{10}$

**Now swim to pages 44–45 to record what you have learned in your explorer's logbook.**

# Length

The measures of **length** we normally use are metric, which means they are based on multiples of 10.

10 millimetres = 1 centimetre
100 cm = 1 metre
1000 m = 1 kilometre

Investigate how to convert from one measure to another.

**Task 1**

1 mile = 1.6 km
Use your calculator to find out how many ...

a  km there are in:        i) 3 miles _____

   ii) 10 miles _____    iii) 25 miles _____

1 inch = 2.54 cm
Use your calculator to find out how many ...

b  cm there are in:        i) 5 inches _____

   ii) 12 inches _____   iii) 20 inches _____

## FACT FILE

**Animal:** Arctic tern
**Habitat:** The waters of the Arctic, Antarctic, Europe, North America and Asia
**Weight:** 86 to 127 g
**Lifespan:** Up to 30 years
**Diet:** Cod and herring, molluscs, crabs, krill, berries and insects

**Task 2**  Change these measures into centimetres.

a  56 mm = _____    b  8 mm = _____

Change these measures into millimetres.

c  7 cm = _____    d  4.3 cm = _____

e  How do you change mm into cm and cm into mm?

_____

_____

**Task 3**  Change these measures into metres.

**a** 671 cm = _____  **b** 701 cm = _____

**c** 1021 cm = _____  **d** 56 cm = _____

Change these measures into centimetres.

**e** 5.93 m = _____  **f** 8.04 m = _____

**g** 11.15 m = _____  **h** 0.82 m = _____

**WILD FACT**

The Arctic tern produces its young in the Northern Hemisphere and then migrates to the other side of the Earth, taking advantage of longer daylight hours in the southern-most parts of the world. This all-round trip can be a distance of around 35 000 km.

**Task 4**  Change these measures into kilometres.

**a** 449 m = _____  **b** 8937 m = _____

**c** 3012 m = _____  **d** 10 512 m = _____

Change these measures into metres.

**e** 5.024 km = _____  **f** 4.001 km = _____

**WILD FACT**

One of the longest recorded migrations is 18 056 km, from Wales to Australia, in just four months!

**Exploring Further ...**

Jenny is building up a fact file on the lengths of various seabirds. She has ordered the birds from smallest to largest but she needs help to order the actual lengths. The birds in her list below are in the right order from smallest to largest. Can you now order the lengths from shortest to longest by converting them to cm? Write the shortest length next to the puffin and so on.

730 mm   0.28 m   0.001 km   0.36 m

Puffin                        _____

Arctic tern                   _____

Macaroni penguin              _____

Black-browed albatross _____

**Now fly to pages 44–45 to record what you have learned in your explorer's logbook.**

# Weight

The measures of **weight** or **mass** we normally use are metric too:

1000 mg (milligrams) = 1 gram
1000 g = 1 kilogram
1000 kg = 1 tonne

Work out how to convert from one to another.
Some imperial measures of weight are pounds and ounces.

## FACT FILE

**Animal:** Hammerhead shark
**Habitat:** In warmer waters worldwide, along coastlines and far offshore
**Weight:** 230 to 450 kg
**Lifespan:** 20 to 30 years
**Diet:** Fish, crustaceans, rays, squid and other sharks

## WILD FACT

The bizarrely-shaped head acts like a metal detector as the shark sweeps the ocean floor looking for prey. It is covered with sensors which pick up the electrical signals given off by fish as they breathe.

**Task 1**   Change these measures into grams.

**a** 6 kg _____

**b** 8.981 kg _____

**c** 3.072 kg _____

**d** 7.003 kg _____

**e** 0.526 kg _____

**f** 1.1 kg _____

**g** How did you change kg into g?

_____

_____

## Task 2

**Now change these measures into kilograms.**

**a** 57 g  _____

**b** 6285 g  _____

**c** 7058 g  _____

**d** 123 g  _____

**e** 890 g  _____

**f** 99 g  _____

## Task 3

**1 pound = 0.45 kg and 1 ounce = 28.3 g**
**Use your calculator to find out how many ...**

**a** kilograms are in:

  **i)** 3 pounds  _____   **ii)** 10 pounds  _____

**b** pounds are in:

  **i)** 9 kg  _____   **ii)** 18 kg  _____   **iii)** 27 kg  _____

**c** grams are in:

  **i)** 2 ounces  _____   **ii)** 10 ounces  _____

**d** ounces are in (round your answers to 2 dp):

  **i)** 50 g  _____   **ii)** 30 g  _____   **iii)** 48 g  _____

### WILD FACT

The shark's eyes are found on the ends of the hammer-like projections on its head, enabling it to have 360° vision.

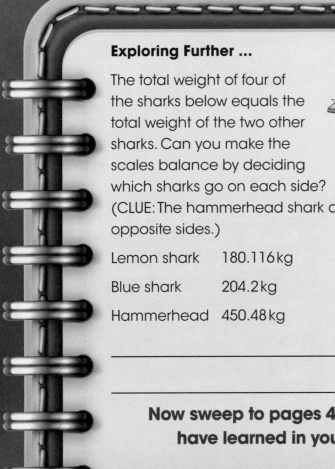

### Exploring Further ...

The total weight of four of the sharks below equals the total weight of the two other sharks. Can you make the scales balance by deciding which sharks go on each side?
(CLUE: The hammerhead shark and the lemon shark should be on opposite sides.)

| | | | |
|---|---|---|---|
| Lemon shark | 180.116 kg | Goblin shark | 266 000 g |
| Blue shark | 204.2 kg | Great white shark | 1.2 t |
| Hammerhead | 450.48 kg | Tiger shark | 1000.164 kg |

_____

_____

**Now sweep to pages 44–45 to record what you have learned in your explorer's logbook.**

# Capacity

## Task 1

**Change these measures into litres.**

a 1000 ml _____

b 6000 ml _____

c 10 000 ml _____

## WILD FACT

The sea squirt can filter up to 200 litres of water every hour at feeding times. If you find one in a tidal pool and gently squeeze it, you will get an eyeful of water!

## Task 2

**Change these measures into litres.**

a 4714 ml = _____

b 8093 ml = _____

c 3002 ml = _____

d 629 ml = _____

e 550 ml = _____

f 26 ml = _____

## FACT FILE

**Animal:** Sea squirt
**Habitat:** Oceans all over the world, usually in shallow water
**Weight:** 100 to 200 g
**Length:** 3 to 30 cm
**Lifespan:** 7 to 30 years
**Diet:** Mainly plankton, nutrients and algae

## Task 3 — Change these measures into millilitres.

**a** 9.153 litres = _____

**b** 7.012 litres = _____

**c** 1.001 litres = _____

**d** 0.612 litres = _____

**e** 0.935 litres = _____

**f** 0.037 litres = _____

## Task 4 — 1 pint = 568 ml. Use your calculator to find out how many . . .

**a** ml there are in:

**i)** 2 pints _____ **ii)** 10 pints _____

**b** pints there are in:

**i)** 852 ml _____ **ii)** 2840 ml _____

**1 gallon = 4.55 litres**
**Use your calculator to find out how many . . .**

**c** litres there are in:

**i)** 2 gallons _____ **ii)** 8 gallons _____

**d** gallons there are in (round your answers to 2 dp):

**i)** 28 litres _____ **ii)** 15 litres _____

### Exploring Further ...

**a** A pet shop owner kept getting his decimal points mixed up. He needed 83.5 litres of sea water but ordered 8.35 litres. How much more did he need? _____

**b** The following day he ordered 42.5 litres instead of 4.25 litres. How much extra did he have? _____

**c** This excess still did not make up the previous day's shortfall. How much more sea water does he still need? Give your answer in millilitres. _____

**Now wriggle to pages 44–45 to record what you have learned in your explorer's logbook.**

# Area and perimeter

**Perimeter** is the total distance *around* the outer edge of a two-dimensional (2D) shape.

The perimeter of a rectangle is:
2 × (length + width)

The perimeter of a square is:
4 × length of side

**Area** is the amount of space *inside* a 2D shape and is measured in square units.

The area of a square and a rectangle is:
length × width

## Task 1

Match each shape with the correct area (A) and perimeter (P). Each square has sides of 1 cm.

a      b      c

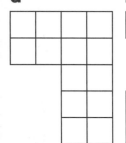
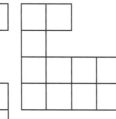
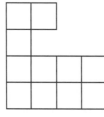

**1** P = 20 cm     A = 11 cm² _____

**2** P = 18 cm     A = 11 cm² _____

**3** P = 18 cm     A = 14 cm² _____

## Task 2
Find the perimeter and area of each of the following rectangles.

| | Length | Width | Perimeter | Area |
|---|---|---|---|---|
| a | 9 cm | 4 cm | | |
| b | 12 cm | 3 cm | | |
| c | 8 cm | 7 cm | | |
| d | 9 cm | 5 cm | | |
| e | 34 cm | 5 cm | | |

## WILD FACT
Flying fish fly to escape from predators. Unfortunately, they can often complete this phenomenal feat only to find themselves landing near the mouth of another predator.

## Task 3
Fill in the missing measurements for these rectangles.

| | Length | Width | Perimeter | Area |
|---|---|---|---|---|
| a | | 4 m | | 28 m² |
| b | 9 m | | | 63 m² |
| c | | 4 m | 24 m | |
| d | 13 m | | 30 m | |

## Task 4
Estimate the area of the following shapes. Each square has sides of 1 cm.

a 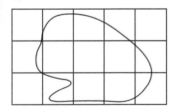     b 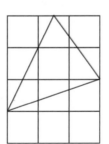     c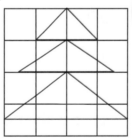

## WILD FACT
Sailors often find flying fish on the decks of their boats some 12 m high.

a _____     b _____     c _____

### Exploring Further ...
James has 24 m of fencing and Sanya has 42 m of fencing. They both wish to mark out a rectangle on the beach with the largest possible area. Investigate and calculate the dimensions of their respective rectangles.

James: _____ m × _____ m     Sanya: _____ m × _____ m

**Now fly to pages 44–45 to record what you have learned in your explorer's logbook.**

# Volume

**Task 1**   Look at this shape.

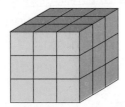

**a** How many small cubes are contained in this shape? _____

Calculate the volume of the shape in cm³ if the small cubes measure:

**b** 2 cm × 2 cm × 2 cm _____

**c** 3 cm × 3 cm × 3 cm _____

**Task 2**   Look at this shape.

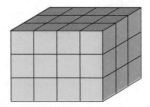

**a** How many small cubes are contained in this shape? _____

Calculate the volume of the shape in cm³ if the small cubes measure:

**b** 2 cm × 2 cm × 2 cm _____

**c** 3 cm × 3 cm × 3 cm _____

## FACT FILE

**Animal:** Puffin

**Habitat:** Open sea, grassy cliff-tops and islands, and boulders at the foot of steep cliffs across the North Atlantic and Arctic Oceans

**Weight:** 500 g

**Lifespan:** Up to 30 years

**Diet:** Fish

**Task 3**  Now look at this shape.

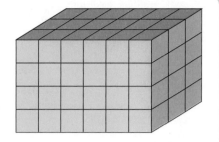

**a** How many small cubes are contained in this shape?

_____

Calculate the volume of the shape in cm³ if the small cubes measure:

**b** 1 cm × 1 cm × 1 cm _____

**c** 2 cm × 2 cm × 2 cm _____

**Task 4**  Calculate the volume of these containers.

**a** 6 m × 5 m × 2 m  _____

**b** 4 m × 3 m × 3 m  _____

**c** 50 cm × 40 cm × 9 cm  _____

**d** 2 m × 2000 mm × 60 cm  _____ m³

**e** 10 mm × 2 cm × 30 mm  _____ cm³

**Exploring Further ...**

1000 litres of water fill 1m³.

A tank measures 600 cm × 8000 mm × 12 m.

How many litres of water will it hold? _____

**Now bob to pages 44–45 to record what you have learned in your explorer's logbook.**

# Time

Measures of **time** are *not* metric as they are determined by the movement of the Earth.

60 seconds = 1 minute

60 minutes = 1 hour

24 hours = 1 day

7 days = 1 week

You need to know the multiples of 60, 24 and 7.

## FACT FILE

**Animal:** Great white shark

**Habitat:** The coastal surface waters of nearly all the world's oceans

**Weight:** 2268 kg (or more)

**Lifespan:** 70 years

**Diet:** Fish, seabirds, seals, sea lions, sea turtles, sea otters and dolphins

---

**Task 1** Convert to minutes, or minutes and seconds.

a    120 seconds  _____

b    180 seconds  _____

c    75 seconds  _____

d    69 seconds  _____

## WILD FACT

The great white shark is the most renowned sea predator. It has 300 triangular saw-like teeth set in rows and if it loses a tooth, a new one appears in its place! Now that's a set of teeth to be wary of!

## Task 2 — Convert to hours, or hours and minutes.

a  240 minutes  _____

b  300 minutes  _____

c  105 minutes  _____

d  84 minutes  _____

## Task 3 — Convert to days.

a  24 hours  _____

b  48 hours  _____

c  72 hours  _____

d  120 hours  _____

## Task 4 — Convert to weeks, or weeks and days.

a  56 days  _____

b  35 days  _____

c  71 days  _____

d  89 days  _____

### Exploring Further ...

A return sea voyage from Sunny Island took 186 days, which was twice as long as the outward journey. The sailors rested for 96 hours on the island.

How many weeks and days did the whole expedition last?

_____

_____

**Now power to pages 44–45 to record what you have learned in your explorer's logbook.**

# 3D shapes

A **3D shape** has volume or capacity. It has three dimensions: length, width and height (depth).

3D shapes are identified by **faces** (flat surfaces), **vertices** (corners) and **edges** (where two faces meet).

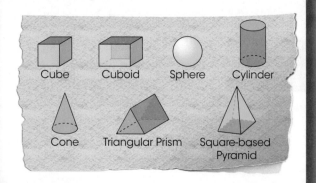

Cube    Cuboid    Sphere    Cylinder

Cone    Triangular Prism    Square-based Pyramid

**Task 1**    Complete the table below.

| Shape | Faces | Edges | Vertices |
|---|---|---|---|
| cube | 6 | | |
| cuboid | | | |
| triangular prism | | | |

**Task 2**    Name each shape.

**a** I have no flat surfaces at all. I am a _____.

**b** I have a circular base and one point. I am a _____.

**c** I have a curved surface and two flat, circular ends.

I am a _____.

## Task 3

**Draw a line to match each shape to its correct name.**

 Triangular-based pyramid

Cone

Cylinder

 Cuboid

Triangular prism

 Sphere

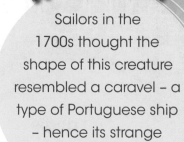

**Exploring Further ...**

Solve the crossword about 3D shapes.

**ACROSS**

1 I am the flat side of a 3D shape.

4 Toilet paper comes wrapped around me.

8 I can have two matching end faces and rectangular sides.

9 I am the line where two faces come together.

10 I am another word for vertices.

**DOWN**

2 I am circular at one end and have a point at the other.

3 My triangular faces come together at a point.

5 Shapes with volume have three _____.

6 I have 12 edges of equal length.

7 I am completely round.

All the letters in the shaded squares can be rearranged to make the name of another 3D shape. What am I?

_____

**Now drift to pages 44–45 to record what you have learned in your explorer's logbook.**

# Angles

An **angle** occurs at the point at which two straight lines meet. Angles are measured in degrees (°).

Angles at a point add up to 360°. Angles on a straight line add up to 180°.

## FACT FILE

| | |
|---|---|
| **Animal:** | Anglerfish |
| **Habitat:** | Open water and sea floors of the Atlantic Ocean, Black Sea and Mediterranean Sea |
| **Weight:** | Up to 50 kg |
| **Lifespan:** | 20 years |
| **Diet:** | Fish, crustaceans, worms and clams |

---

**Task 1**  Choose from the following options to describe each angle:

right angle          obtuse          reflex          acute

a          b          c          d          e

## Task 2

Calculate the missing angles using the information given.

**a**

**b**

**c**

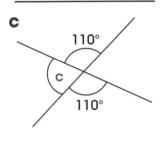

**d**

## Task 3

True or false? Circle the right answer.

**a** There are 180° in a circle.      True / False
**b** An angle of 85° is obtuse.      True / False
**c** A rectangle has four right angles.      True / False
**d** A reflex angle is greater than 180°.      True / False
**e** A right angle is 45°.      True / False

### Exploring Further ...

Help Pirate Pete find his treasure! He starts off in the square shown on the grid, facing north. Follow the instructions and put a cross in the square where the treasure can be found.

1 Turn 180°. Move 1 square forward.
2 Turn 90° clockwise. Move 2 squares forward.
3 Turn 270° clockwise. Move 2 squares forward.
4 Turn 90° anti-clockwise. Move 1 square forward.
5 Turn 45° anti-clockwise. Move 1 square forward.
6 Turn 90° anti-clockwise. Move 3 squares forward.

You've found the treasure – start digging!

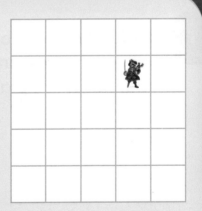

**Now swim to pages 44–45 to record what you have learned in your explorer's logbook.**

# Transformations

**Reflection** and **translation** describe changes in a shape's position, but the shape keeps the same size. When a shape is reflected, it 'flips' over to give a mirror reflection. When a shape is translated, it merely 'slides' to its new place. **Transformation** describes how a shape changes position.

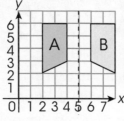

B is a reflection of A in the line $x = 5$

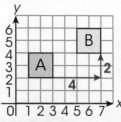

B is a translation of A by the vector $\begin{pmatrix} 4 \\ 2 \end{pmatrix}$

**Task 1** State whether each transformation of A to B below is a reflection or a translation, and describe the transformation that has taken place.

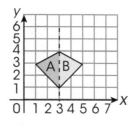

**a**

_____

_____

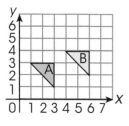

**b**

_____

_____

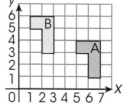

**c**

_____

_____

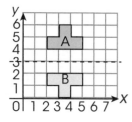

**d**

_____

_____

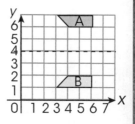

**e**

_____

_____

## FACT FILE

**Animal:** Dugong
**Habitat:** The shallow waters around North Australia, south-east Asia and the eastern coast of Africa
**Weight:** 230 to 500 kg
**Lifespan:** Up to 80 years
**Diet:** Seagrass

## WILD FACT

Have you ever heard of a dugong? Related to the elephant, they gave rise to the myth about mermaids. Sailors, after months at sea, would think they were beautiful maidens out for a swim!

## WILD FACT

The dugong eats up to 50 kg of seagrass per day. Seagrass, however, is not easily digested. So to prevent indigestion, the dugong has an intestine which is 30 m long and as thick as a firefighter's hosepipe.

### Task 2    Carry out these transformations.

**a** Reflect this shape in the line $y = 3$

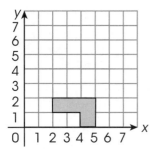

**b** Reflect this shape in the line $x = 4$

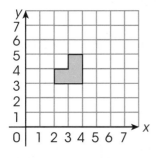

**c** Redraw this shape after a translation of $\binom{3}{2}$

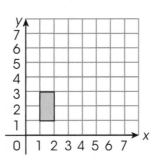

**d** Redraw this shape after a translation of $\binom{-2}{3}$

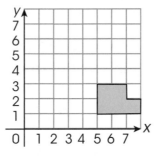

### Exploring Further ...

Reflect this shape in the dotted line. Label the new shape A.

Redraw the original shape after a translation of $\binom{1}{0}$

Redraw shape A after a translation of $\binom{-1}{0}$

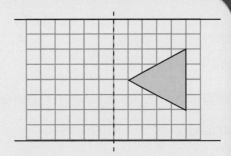

**Now glide to pages 44–45 to record what you have learned in your explorer's logbook.**

# Statistics

**Statistics** is an exciting part of maths. Statistics involves collecting, organising, representing and analysing **data**. Often data is organised in a **table**. It may then be presented as a **graph**. Graphs enable us to see the information more clearly and to analyse it objectively.

## FACT FILE

**Animal:** Plankton

**Habitat:** Oceans all over the world

**Diet:** Some plankton photosynthesise; other plankton eat bacteria and detritus or smaller plankton

---

**Task 1**   Elray conducted a survey of porpoise sightings in the bay near his home. This table shows his results.

| Day | Tally marks | Total |
|-----|-------------|-------|
| Monday | |||| | |
| Tuesday | ||||| | |
| Wednesday | ||||| ||| | |
| Thursday | | 10 |
| Friday | | 3 |
| Saturday | | 0 |
| Sunday | ||||| ||||| || | |

a  Complete the table.

b  On which day were there most sightings? _____

c  On which day was there no sighting? _____

d  How many sightings were there on Wednesday? _____

e  How many sightings were there altogether? _____

f  Complete this sentence:

Elray made six more sightings on _____ than on _____.

## Task 2

Humpback whales eat lots of plankton. This graph shows the number of humpback whales seen from 2008–2014.

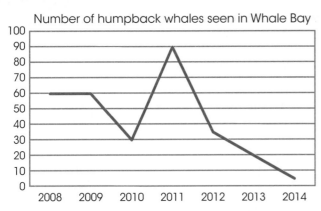

Number of humpback whales seen in Whale Bay

**a** In which year did the numbers of humpback whales peak?

_____

**b** How many whales were seen in 2010?

_____

**c** What is the difference between the numbers in 2011 and 2014? (Specify whether it is an increase or decrease.)

_____

**d** What does the graph tell us about the numbers of humpback whales?

_____

### Exploring Further ...

Here is some information on four types of whale.

| Sperm | Length 18 m | Weight 50 t |
|-------|-------------|-------------|
| Minke | Length 10 m | Weight 10 t |
| Pilot | Length 6 m | Weight 4 t |
| Killer | Length 10 m | Weight 9 t |

Draw a bar chart to represent the information given on length and weight. Show two bars for each whale – one for length and one for weight.

**Now drift to pages 44–45 to record what you have learned in your explorer's logbook.**

**WILD FACT**

'Zooplankton' is the term which describes the large number of tiny, invertebrate animals which live in the sea. All other sea creatures depend upon a plentiful supply of zooplankton.

# Quick test

Now try these questions. Give yourself 1 mark for every correct answer – but only if you answer each part of the question correctly.

**1** Take two hundred and ninety-six thousand nine hundred and eighty-nine from six hundred and twenty-four thousand and seventy-two.

**2** The numbers in this diagram are all whole numbers greater than 1. The number in each circle is the product of the numbers in the squares connected to it.
Fill in the missing numbers.

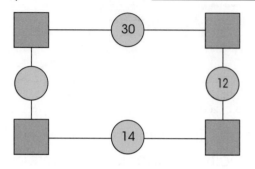

**3** Complete this table.

| Shape | Faces | Edges | Vertices |
|---|---|---|---|
| Cube | 6 | 12 | 8 |
| Square-based pyramid | | | |
| Hexagonal prism | | | |
| Triangular-based pyramid | | | |
| Triangular prism | | | |

**4** 274 × 36 = 9864
Use this information to find the answer to this sum: ? × 36 = 98.64

**5** Use these digits to make the closest possible number to 600 000.
6    5    1    8    3    7

**6** Sea level is at 0 m, the Arctic tern is flying at 10 m and the sea otter is swimming at –5 m.
What is the distance between the sea otter and the Arctic tern?

**7** Write the missing numbers in this sequence:
56    49    43    38    34    31    ____    ____

**8** Bob and Haziq collected shells on the beach and shared them between themselves, Tariq and Jim. Bob got $\frac{2}{5}$, Haziq got $\frac{3}{10}$ and Tariq got $\frac{3}{25}$.

**a** What fraction did Jim receive?

**b** Who received most shells?

**9** A blue whale weighs 154 852 kg.
Round its weight to the nearest 10, 100 and 1000 kg.

**10** Sea Life World sells postcards of sea creatures. Postcards are priced according to area. Postcards with the same area cost the same. The cost is in proportion to the area, so a postcard with an area of 20 cm² costs twice as much as one with an area of 10 cm². Complete this price list:

| Size | Price |
|---|---|
| 5 cm × 4 cm | 60 p |
| 10 cm × | 60 p |
| 8 cm × 5 cm | |
| 5 cm × | 30 p |
| 5 cm × | £1.80 |

**11** Look at the diagram below.

   **a**  Measure the acute angle marked x with a protractor.    _____

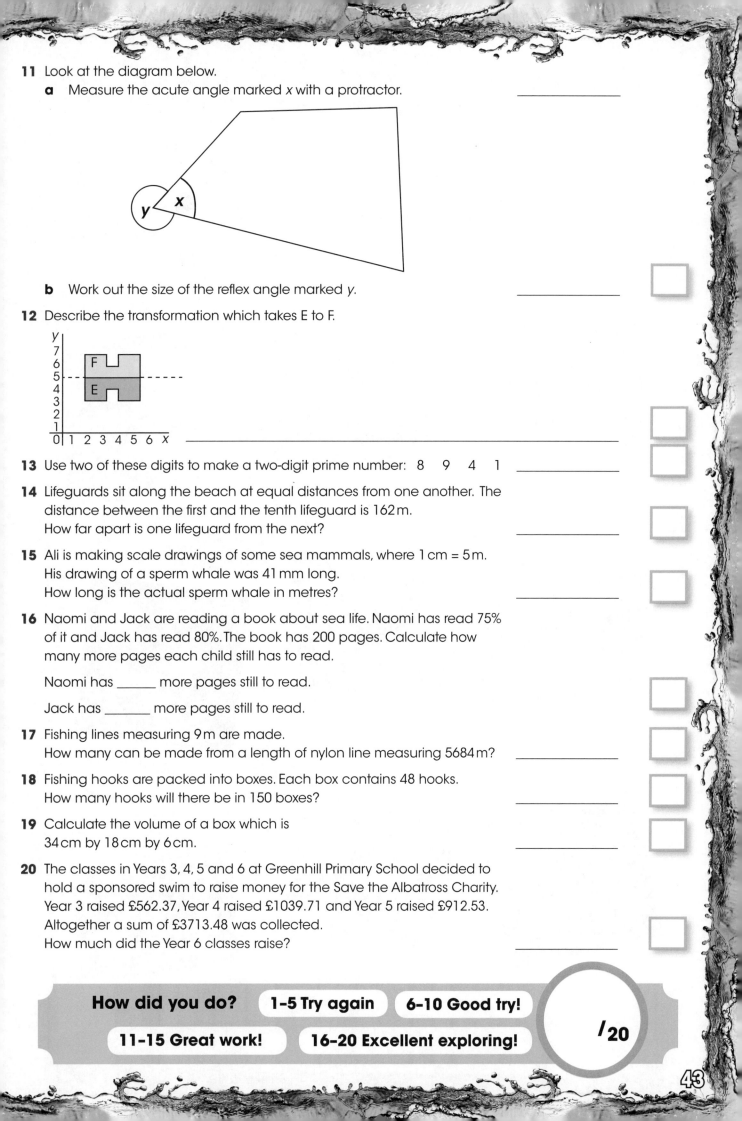

   **b**  Work out the size of the reflex angle marked y.    _____ ☐

**12** Describe the transformation which takes E to F.

_____ ☐

**13** Use two of these digits to make a two-digit prime number:  8  9  4  1  _____ ☐

**14** Lifeguards sit along the beach at equal distances from one another. The
distance between the first and the tenth lifeguard is 162m.
How far apart is one lifeguard from the next?    _____ ☐

**15** Ali is making scale drawings of some sea mammals, where 1cm = 5m.
His drawing of a sperm whale was 41mm long.
How long is the actual sperm whale in metres?    _____ ☐

**16** Naomi and Jack are reading a book about sea life. Naomi has read 75%
of it and Jack has read 80%. The book has 200 pages. Calculate how
many more pages each child still has to read.

   Naomi has _____ more pages still to read.

   Jack has _____ more pages still to read. ☐

**17** Fishing lines measuring 9m are made.
How many can be made from a length of nylon line measuring 5684m?  _____ ☐

**18** Fishing hooks are packed into boxes. Each box contains 48 hooks.
How many hooks will there be in 150 boxes?    _____ ☐

**19** Calculate the volume of a box which is
34cm by 18cm by 6cm.    _____ ☐

**20** The classes in Years 3, 4, 5 and 6 at Greenhill Primary School decided to
hold a sponsored swim to raise money for the Save the Albatross Charity.
Year 3 raised £562.37, Year 4 raised £1039.71 and Year 5 raised £912.53.
Altogether a sum of £3713.48 was collected.
How much did the Year 6 classes raise?    _____ ☐

**How did you do?**   1–5 Try again   6–10 Good try!

**11–15 Great work!**   16–20 Excellent exploring!   **/20**

# Explorer's Logbook

Tick off the topics as you complete them and then colour in the star.

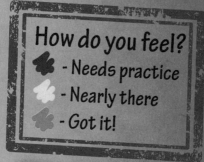
How do you feel?
- Needs practice
- Nearly there
- Got it!

Transformations ☐

Area and perimeter ☐

Fractions ☐

Subtraction ☐

Place value ☐

Multiplication ☐

Division ☐

Weight ☐

3D shapes ☐

Percentages ☐

Number knowledge ☐

Addition ☐

Decimals ☐

Capacity ☐

Volume ☐

Length ☐

Time ☐

Angles ☐

Rounding numbers ☐

Statistics ☐

# Answers

**Pages 2–3**

**Task 1**
a  1 000 000          b  850 005          c  46 460

**Task 2**
a  one hundred and seventy-eight thousand
b  nine hundred and four thousand three hundred and ninety

**Task 3**
a  999 090, 991 099, 990 090, 990 009, 909 009
b  786 463, 786 462, 785 642, 758 462, 758 246
c  505 005, 505 055, 550 505, 555 050, 555 555
d  10 999, 100 004, 100 304, 100 403, 101 001

**Task 4**
a  **9346**    9246    9146    **9046**    **8946**
   8846    **8746**
b  435 653    **535 653**    635 653    735 653    **835 653**
   **935 653**    **1 035 653**

**Exploring Further …**
a  25 000 mm          b  177 998 kg          c  147 998 kg

**Pages 4–5**

**Task 1**
a  260          b  134 440          c  4700          d  17 700

**Task 2**
a  4000          b  54 000          c  50 000          d  10 000

**Task 3**
a  100 000          b  300 000

**Task 4**
a  14          b  3          c  −2°

**Exploring Further …**
a  5 to 14          b  50 to 149          c  145 000 to 154 999

**Pages 6–7**

**Task 1**
a  81          b  141          c  9989
d  473          e  1100

**Task 2**
a  70 cm          b  65 kg          c  95 m

**Task 3**
a  25 010          b  784

**Exploring Further …**
a  87 261          b  104 560
c  48 000 + 40 000 + 17 000 = 105 000

**Pages 8–9**

**Task 1**
a  43          b  232          c  2540          d  415
e  574          f  182          g  66          h  236
i  468

**Task 2**
a  176 cm          b  2021 km          c  1750

**Task 3**
a  263          b  2132          c  15 872
d  14 772          e  155 368          f  438 842

**Exploring Further …**
a  A flew 416 910 km          B flew 440 261 km
b  B flew further
c  By 23 351 km

**Pages 10–11**

**Task 1**
a  56, 48, 96          b  35, 63, 49, 21
c  54, 72, 18, 36          d  12, 24

**Task 2**
a  1, 2, 3, 6, 9, 18     b  1, 2, 4, 8, 16, 32     c  1, 2, 3, 4, 6, 12

**Task 3**
a  36, 64, 4          b  1000, 8, 64          c  37, 29, 97, 2
d  $6^2 - 3^2 = 3^3$          e  $5^2 - 4^2 = 3^2$

**Exploring Further …**
a  Incorrect  $9 \times 15 = 3^2 \times (3 \times 5) = 3^3 \times 5$
b  Correct
c  Incorrect  $25 \times 10 = 5^2 \times (5 \times 2) = 5^3 \times 2$
d  Incorrect  $12 \times 360 = (4 \times 3) \times (4 \times 9 \times 10) =$
                    $4^2 \times 3^3 \times 10$
e  Incorrect  $54 \times 18 = (3^2 \times 6) \times (6 \times 3) = 3^3 \times 6^2$

**Pages 12–13**

**Task 1**
a  i) 12          ii) 14          iii) 24          iv) 36
b  i) 35          ii) 54          iii) 15          iv) 24
c  i) 56          ii) 49          iii) 72          iv) 40
d  i) 27          ii) 63          iii) 48          iv) 42

**Task 2**
a  1386 g          b  450

**Task 3**
a  i) 235          ii) 4842          iii) 65 648
b  i) 774          ii) 1080          iii) 19 158
c  i) 3886          ii) 9116          iii) 359 250

**Exploring Further …**
a  35 × 60 = 2100 times
b  35 × 75 = 2625 times
c  2100 (answer to a) × 60 = 126 000 times

**Pages 14–15**

**Task 1**
a  i) $\frac{1}{2} = \frac{2}{4}$    ii) $\frac{3}{4} = \frac{6}{8}$    iii) $\frac{4}{5} = \frac{8}{10}$    iv) $\frac{4}{6} = \frac{2}{3}$
b  $\frac{1}{2} = \frac{2}{4} = \frac{3}{6} = \frac{4}{8} = \frac{5}{10} = \frac{50}{100}$
c  $\frac{1}{4} = \frac{2}{8} = \frac{25}{100}$
d  i) $\frac{1}{2} < \frac{4}{5}$    ii) $\frac{7}{8} > \frac{8}{10}$    iii) $\frac{3}{4} = \frac{75}{100}$

**Task 2**
a  i) $1\frac{2}{5}$    ii) $1\frac{3}{6} = 1\frac{1}{2}$          b  i) $\frac{7}{4}$    ii) $\frac{14}{5}$

**Task 3**
a  i) $\frac{3}{5}$    ii) $\frac{7}{6} = 1\frac{1}{6}$          b  i) $\frac{2}{9}$    ii) $\frac{3}{7}$
c  i) $\frac{7}{10}$    ii) $\frac{13}{8} = 1\frac{5}{8}$          d  i) $\frac{2}{15}$    ii) $\frac{5}{9}$

**Exploring Further …**
a  Squares shaded
   i) 6    ii) 15    iii) 8    iv) 7    v) 10    vi) 12    vii) 5
b  $\frac{63}{36} = 1$ whole one and $\frac{27}{36} = 1\frac{3}{4}$          c  $\frac{9}{36} = \frac{1}{4}$

**Pages 16–17**

**Task 1**
a  i) 7    ii) 12          b  i) 11    ii) 3          c  i) 9    ii) 9
d  i) 5    ii) 5          e  i) 40    ii) 8          f  i) 7    ii) 6
g  i) 9    ii) 4          h  i) 8    ii) 1

**Task 2**
a  105          b  3769 r1          c  1204 r2

**Task 3**
a  46 ÷ 6 = 7 r4  8 boats are needed.
b  2450 l ÷ 4 = 612 r2 litres = $612\frac{2}{4}$ = $612\frac{1}{2}$ litres

**Exploring Further …**
a  23 ÷ 5 = 4 r3          b  64 ÷ 5 = 12 r4          c  24 ÷ 5 = 4 r4

**Pages 18–19**

**Task 1**
a  i) 20          ii) 8          iii) 350
b  i) 63          ii) 2          iii) 40
c  i) 736          ii) 150          iii) 600

**Task 2**
a  i) 830          ii) 410          iii) 400
b  i) 4.1          ii) 8.1          iii) 6.0

**Task 3**
a  i) $\frac{1}{10}$          ii) $\frac{3}{10}$          iii) $\frac{8}{10}$ or $\frac{4}{5}$
b  i) $\frac{37}{100}$          ii) $\frac{18}{100}$ or $\frac{9}{50}$          iii) $\frac{5}{100}$ or $\frac{1}{20}$
c  i) $\frac{951}{1000}$          ii) $\frac{13}{1000}$          iii) $\frac{4}{1000}$ or $\frac{2}{500}$ or $\frac{1}{250}$
d  i) 0.5          ii) 0.4          iii) 0.9
e  i) 0.32          ii) 0.56          iii) 0.02
f  i) 0.691          ii) 0.043          iii) 0.006

**Task 4**
a  i) 85.8          ii) 0.55          b  i) 8          ii) 5.05
c  2.915, 2.591, 2.059, 2.058, 2.008
d  4.21, 3.9, 3.841, 3.84, 3.814

**Exploring Further …**
a  1.7          b  4.05          c  1.2          d  8.05

**Pages 20–21**

**Task 1**
a  i) 0.43          ii) 0.59          iii) 0.4          iv) 0.93
b  i) 0.01          ii) 0.04          iii) 0.07          iv) 0.09
c  i) 18%          ii) 42%          iii) 68%          iv) 20%
d  i) 2%          ii) 3%          iii) 5%          iv) 6%

**Task 2**

**a** i) $\frac{13}{100}$  ii) $\frac{27}{100}$  iii) $\frac{50}{100}$

**b** i) $\frac{2}{100}$  ii) $\frac{3}{100}$  iii) $\frac{6}{100}$

**c** i) 15%  ii) 34%  iii) 90%

**d** i) 4%  ii) 9%  iii) 7%

**Task 3**

**a** i) $\frac{1}{10} = \frac{10}{100} = 10\%$  ii) $\frac{3}{10} = \frac{30}{100} = 30\%$

**b** i) $\frac{1}{5} = \frac{2}{10} = \frac{20}{100} = 20\%$  ii) $\frac{4}{5} = \frac{8}{10} = \frac{80}{100} = 80\%$

**c** i) $\frac{1}{2} = \frac{5}{10} = \frac{50}{100} = 50\%$  ii) $\frac{1}{4} = \frac{25}{100} = 25\%$

**Exploring Further ...**

**a** $\frac{2}{5}$, $\frac{3}{10}$, 10%, $\frac{1}{5}$

**b** 23%, 0.07, 0.45, $\frac{1}{4}$

**Pages 22–23**

**Task 1**

**a** i) 4.8 km  ii) 16 km  iii) 40 km

**b** i) 12.7 cm  ii) 30.48 cm  iii) 50.8 cm

**Task 2**

**a** 5.6 cm

**b** 0.8 cm

**c** 70 mm

**d** 43 mm

**e** To change mm into cm ÷ by 10
   To change cm into mm × by 10

**Task 3**

**a** 6.71 m  **b** 7.01 m  **c** 10.21 m

**d** 0.56 m  **e** 593 cm  **f** 804 cm

**g** 1115 cm  **h** 82 cm

**Task 4**

**a** 0.449 km  **b** 8.937 km  **c** 3.012 km

**d** 10.512 km  **e** 5024 m  **f** 4001 m

**Exploring Further ...**

Puffin                        0.28 m = 28 cm

Arctic tern                  0.36 m = 36 cm

Macaroni penguin       730 mm = 73 cm

Black-browed albatross  0.001 km = 100 cm

**Pages 24–25**

**Task 1**

**a** 6000 g  **b** 8981 g  **c** 3072 g

**d** 7003 g  **e** 526 g  **f** 1100 g

**g** To change kilograms into grams × by 1000

**Task 2**

**a** 0.057 kg  **b** 6.285 kg  **c** 7.058 kg

**d** 0.123 kg  **e** 0.890 kg  **f** 0.099 kg

**Task 3**

**a** i) 1.35 kg  ii) 4.5 kg

**b** i) 20 lb  ii) 40 lb  iii) 60 lb

**c** i) 56.6 g  ii) 283 g

**d** i) 1.77 oz  ii) 1.06 oz  iii) 1.70 oz

**Exploring Further ...**

Blue + Tiger + Lemon + Goblin = Great white + Hammerhead

**Pages 26–27**

**Task 1**

**a** 1 litre  **b** 6 litres  **c** 10 litres

**Task 2**

**a** 4.714 litres  **b** 8.093 litres  **c** 3.002 litres

**d** 0.629 litres  **e** 0.550 litres  **f** 0.026 litres

**Task 3**

**a** 9153 ml  **b** 7012 ml  **c** 1001 ml

**d** 612 ml  **e** 935 ml  **f** 37 ml

**Task 4**

**a** i) 1136 ml  **b** i) 1.5 pints  **c** i) 9.1 litres  **d** i) 6.15 gallons
   ii) 5680 ml      ii) 5 pints      ii) 36.4 litres      ii) 3.30 gallons

**Exploring Further ...**

**a** 83.5 – 8.35 = 75.15 litres

**b** 42.5 – 4.25 = 38.25 litres

**c** 75.15 – 38.25 = 36.9 litres = 36 900 ml

**Pages 28–29**

**Task 1**

**a** 3  **b** 1  **c** 2

**Task 2**

**a** P = 26 cm A = 36 cm²  **b** P = 30 cm A = 36 cm²

**c** P = 30 cm A = 56 cm²  **d** P = 28 cm A = 45 cm²

**e** P = 78 cm A = 170 cm²

**Task 3**

| | Length | Width | Perimeter | Area |
|---|---|---|---|---|
| **a** | 7 m | 4 m | 22 m | 28 m² |
| **b** | 9 m | 7 m | 32 m | 63 m² |
| **c** | 8 m | 4 m | 24 m | 32 m² |
| **d** | 13 m | 2 m | 30 m | 26 m² |

**Task 4**

**a** Approx 8 cm²  **b** 3.5 cm²–4 cm²

**c** 5.5 cm²–6 cm²

**Exploring Further ...**

James 7 m × 5 m

Sanya 11 m × 10 m

**Pages 30–31**

**Task 1**

**a** 27 cubes  **b** 216 cm³  **c** 729 cm³

**Task 2**

**a** 36 cubes  **b** 288 cm³  **c** 972 cm³

**Task 3**

**a** 72 cubes  **b** 72 cm³  **c** 576 cm³

**Task 4**

**a** 60 m³  **b** 36 m³  **c** 18 000 cm³  **d** 2.4 m³  **e** 6 cm³

**Exploring Further ...**

The tank will hold 576 000 litres of water

**Pages 32–33**

**Task 1**

**a** 2 mins  **b** 3 mins  **c** 1 min 15 secs  **d** 1 min 9 secs

**Task 2**

**a** 4 hrs  **b** 5 hrs  **c** 1 hr 45 mins  **d** 1 hr 24 mins

**Task 3**

**a** 1 day  **b** 2 days  **c** 3 days  **d** 5 days

**Task 4**

**a** 8 wks  **b** 5 wks  **c** 10 wks 1 day  **d** 12 wks 5 days

**Exploring Further ...**

Return journey = 186 days

Outward journey = 186 ÷ 2 = 93 days

Resting time = 96 hrs = 4 days

Total expedition time = 186 + 93 + 4 = 283 days

= 283 ÷ 7

= 40 wks and 3 days

**Pages 34–35**

**Task 1**

| cube | 6 faces | 12 edges | 8 vertices |
|---|---|---|---|
| cuboid | 6 faces | 12 edges | 8 vertices |
| triangular prism | 5 faces | 9 edges | 6 vertices |

**Task 2**

**a** sphere  **b** cone  **c** cylinder

**Task 3**

Triangular-based pyramid      Cone      Cylinder

Cuboid      Sphere      Triangular prism

**Exploring Further ...**

| ACROSS | DOWN |
|---|---|
| 1 face | 2 cone |
| 4 cylinder | 3 pyramid |
| 8 prism | 5 dimensions |
| 9 edge | 6 cube |
| 10 corners | 7 sphere |

What am I? = cuboid

**Pages 36–37**

**Task 1**

**a** obtuse  **b** right angle  **c** acute  **d** obtuse  **e** reflex

**Task 2**

**a** 180° – 45° = 135° (angles on a straight line)

**b** 75° + 30° = 105°
   180° – 105° = 75° (angles on a straight line)

**c** 110° + 110° = 220°
   360° – 220° = 140° (angles at a point)
   140° ÷ 2 = 70° (opposite angles are equal)

**d** 100° + 135° = 235°
   360° – 235° = 125° (angles at a point)

**Task 3**

**a** False. There are 360° in a circle.

**b** False. An angle less than 90° is acute.

**c** True  **d** True

**e** False. A right angle is 90°.

**Exploring Further ...**
Cross at 1,5 (top left square of grid)
**Pages 38–39**
**Task 1**
**a** B is a reflection of A in the line $x = 3$

**b** B is a translation of A by the vector $\begin{pmatrix} 3 \\ 1 \end{pmatrix}$

**c** B is a translation of A by the vector $\begin{pmatrix} -4 \\ 2 \end{pmatrix}$

**d** B is a reflection of A in the line $y = 3$
**e** B is a reflection of A in the line $y = 4$
**Task 2**

**a** 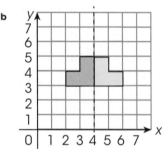 **c**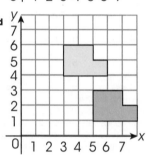

**b** **d**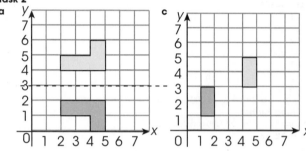

**Exploring Further ...**

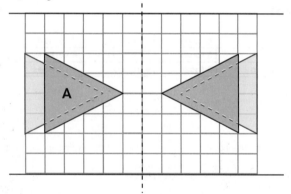

**Pages 40–41**
**Task 1**
**a**

| Day | Tally Marks | Total |
|---|---|---|
| Monday | \|\|\|\| | 4 |
| Tuesday | Ⅲℍ | 5 |
| Wednesday | ℍℍ \|\|\| | 8 |
| Thursday | ℍℍ ℍℍ | 10 |
| Friday | \|\|\| | 3 |
| Saturday | | 0 |
| Sunday | ℍℍ ℍℍ \|\| | 12 |

**b** Sunday    **c** Saturday    **d** 8    **e** 42
**f** Elray made six more sightings on Thursday than on Monday.
**Task 2**
**a** 2011    **b** 30    **c** Decrease of 85
**d** Overall numbers of humpback whales in Whale Bay are decreasing.
**Exploring Further ...**

Any suitable graph, e.g.

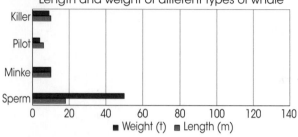

Length and weight of different types of whale

**Quick test answers**
**1** 624 072 – 296 989 = 327 083
**2**

5 — 30 — 6
35      12
7 — 14 — 2

**3**

| Shape | Faces | Edges | Vertices |
|---|---|---|---|
| Cube | 6 | 12 | 8 |
| Square-based pyramid | **5** | **8** | **5** |
| Hexagonal prism | **8** | **18** | **12** |
| Triangular-based pyramid | **4** | **6** | **4** |
| Triangular prism | **5** | **9** | **6** |

**4** **2.74** $\times$ 36 = 98.64   (100x smaller)
**5** 587 631 is closer to 600 000 than 613 578
**6** 15m
**7** 29, 28
**8** **a** Jim received $\frac{18}{100} = \frac{9}{50}$    **b** Bob
**9** 154 850 kg    154 900 kg    155 000 kg
**10**

| Size | Price |
|---|---|
| 5 cm x 4 cm | 60 p |
| 10 cm x **2 cm** | 60 p |
| 8 cm x 5 cm | **£1.20** |
| 5 cm x **2 cm** | 30 p |
| 5 cm x **12 cm** | £1.80 |

**11** **a** 60°    **b** 300°
**12** F is a reflection of E in the line $y = 5$
**13** 89 or 19 or 41
**14** 162 ÷ 9 = 18 m (There are 9 spaces between 10 lifeguards.)
**15** 41 mm = 4.1 cm. 4.1 x 5 = 20.5 The sperm whale is 20.5 m long.
**16** Naomi has **50** more pages still to read.
     Jack has **40** more pages still to read.
**17** 631 lines
**18** 7200 hooks
**19** 3672 cm³
**20** £1198.87